Options Income Made Simple

Book 2: Cash-Secured Puts

How to Use Cash-Secured Puts to Collect Premiums

by Adrian Gregory

For permission requests, contact:

Adrian.gregory@secondsightbraille.com

ISBN: 979-8-9938323-2-6

Printed in the United States of America

The information in this book is provided for educational and informational purposes only and should not be construed as financial, investment, or trading advice. The author is not a licensed financial advisor, broker, or accountant. Options trading involves risk and is not suitable for all investors. You should consult with a qualified financial professional before making any investment decisions.

Neither the author nor the publisher shall be liable for any loss or damages resulting from the use of the information contained in this book. The reader assumes all responsibility for their own financial decisions.

Table of Contents

To Megan, Ellie, and Everly,

Thank you for inspiring me to keep learning, teaching, and building a future worth working for.

Also check out book 1:

Covered Calls For Working People:
Earn Weekly Income with Options

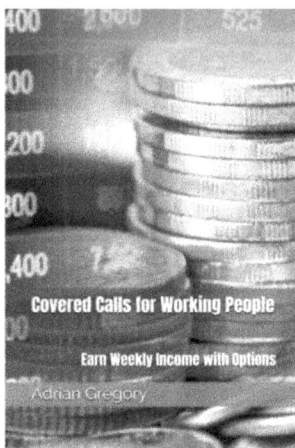

Preface

Options can seem intimidating at first glance. When I first started, I was overwhelmed by charts, jargon, and strategies that felt like they were written for Wall Street professionals, not everyday people. But what I quickly discovered is that some strategies are not only simple, but also practical for generating steady income — without taking on the high risks most people associate with options.

This book is about one of those strategies: **the cash-secured put.** It is the foundation of what's often called *The Wheel Strategy*, and it pairs perfectly with covered calls. In fact, if you've already read my book on covered calls, you'll see how this volume is the natural next step. If you're brand new, don't worry — we'll start from scratch and build your understanding step by step.

My goal in writing this is to take something that can sound complex and make it clear, simple, and actionable. You don't need a finance degree. You don't need insider access. What you need is a plan, patience, and the willingness to learn.

By the end of this book, you'll know:

- What a cash-secured put is and why it's safer than many other options strategies.

- How to set up your account and place your first trade.

- The rules I personally follow to choose stocks, strikes, and expirations.

- How to manage your positions if things don't go as expected.

- And how this strategy connects with covered calls to create reliable income.

This is not financial advice, and I'm not here to promise you instant wealth. But if you take the time to learn and apply these principles, you'll have a tool you can use for the rest of your investing life.

Thank you for reading, and I hope this book helps you take your next step toward building steady, consistent income.

— Adrian Gregory

Introduction: What Is a Cash-Secured Put?

At its core, a **cash-secured put (CSP)** is one of the simplest options strategies you can learn. The name might sound complicated, but once you break it down, it's really just this:

- You **agree to buy a stock** you like, at a price you're comfortable with.

- In return, someone pays you **cash up front** (called a premium).

- You set aside enough cash in your account to make that purchase if it happens.

That's it. You're basically getting **paid to wait** for a good deal on a stock.

Think of it this way: if you've ever told yourself, *"I'll buy this stock if it drops to a certain price,"* then you've already thought like a CSP trader. The difference is, with cash-secured puts, you can **collect income while waiting** for that price to hit.

A Simple Example

Let's say you want to own a stock currently trading at $52, but you'd only be happy buying it at $50.

- You sell a **$50 put option**.

- You receive, for example, **$2 per share in premium** ($200 per contract, since each option covers 100 shares).

- You set aside $5,000 in cash (100 shares × $50 strike).

Two outcomes are possible:

1. **The stock stays above $50.**

   o   Your option expires worthless.

   o   You keep the $200 premium as profit.

   o   You can repeat the process.

2. **The stock drops below $50.**

   o   You're required to buy 100 shares at $50.

   o   But you still keep the $200 premium.

   o   Your effective cost is now $48 per share ($50 – $2 premium).

Either way, you've earned money—and either you get paid to wait, or you buy the stock you wanted at a discount.

Why "Cash-Secured"?

The "cash-secured" part means you keep enough money in your account to *actually buy* the shares if assigned. This makes the strategy safer than selling "naked" puts (which can be very risky). With CSPs, you know exactly how much money is at stake, and your risk is capped at the cash you set aside.

Why Start Here?

Cash-secured puts are one of the **entry-level building blocks** of options income. They're the first half of the Wheel Strategy (puts first, then covered calls). They're also flexible—you can use them to:

- Generate steady monthly income.

- Enter stocks at better prices.

- Build long-term positions without chasing.

In the chapters ahead, we'll go deeper: choosing stocks, picking strikes, managing trades, avoiding mistakes, and connecting it all to the Wheel. But for now, remember this: **a cash-secured put is simply getting paid to agree to buy a stock at your price.**

(Book 1 I did on covered calls. It is where I started, and made the shares I already owned work for me.)

Chapter 1: The Wheel Strategy Explained

The **Wheel Strategy** is one of the most practical, beginner-friendly ways to use options. It's called "the wheel" because it repeats in a cycle, rolling forward step by step, generating income along the way.

At its heart, the Wheel is made up of two simple strategies:

1. **Selling cash-secured puts** (the first half).

2. **Selling covered calls** (the second half).

Put them together, and you have a system that can generate income month after month — while either buying or selling stock at prices you already chose in advance.

Step 1: Sell a Cash-Secured Put

- You agree to buy a stock at a lower price.

- You collect premium up front.

- If the stock never drops, you keep the cash and repeat.

- If the stock falls and you're assigned, you buy shares at a discount.

This is where the Wheel starts. You're either earning money while waiting, or you're acquiring shares of a stock you wanted to own anyway.

Step 2: Own the Shares (if Assigned)

If the put option you sold is assigned, you'll now own 100 shares of the stock. But remember: you wanted those shares, and you got them at the strike price minus the premium you collected. This is often a better deal than if you had just bought the stock directly.

Step 3: Sell a Covered Call

Now that you own the stock, you can sell a **covered call** against it. This means:

- You agree to sell your 100 shares at a higher strike price.

- You collect another premium up front.

- If the stock never reaches that strike, you keep both the shares and the premium.

- If the stock rises above your strike and your shares are called away, you sell them at a profit and still keep the premium.

Step 4: Repeat the Wheel

Once your shares are sold, you're back to cash. And with that cash, you can start again by selling another cash-secured put. The wheel turns, and the cycle repeats.

Why the Wheel Works for Everyday Investors

The Wheel Strategy appeals to regular investors because it's:

- **Simple:** Only two basic option strategies are involved.

- **Flexible:** You can choose your stocks, strike prices, and expirations.

- **Income-Generating:** You collect premium at each stage.

- **Lower Risk than Naked Options:** You're always cash-secured or covered.

Example in Motion

- You sell a put on Stock XYZ with a strike at $50 and collect $200.

- The stock dips and you're assigned, buying 100 shares at $50.

- Next, you sell a covered call at $55 and collect another $200.

- If the stock rises and your shares are sold at $55, you pocket the $500 stock gain + $400 total premiums.

- Now you're back to cash, ready to repeat.

This steady cycle is why so many retail investors call the Wheel one of the **most consistent income strategies in options trading**. And it all begins with understanding the first spoke of the wheel — the **cash-secured put.**

Chapter 2: Account Setup & Requirements

Before you sell your first cash-secured put, you need to make sure your brokerage account is set up correctly. This isn't complicated, but it's important to do it right so you can trade safely and smoothly.

Brokerage Account Type

Most major brokers (Fidelity, Schwab, E*TRADE, TD Ameritrade, Robinhood, Webull, etc.) allow cash-secured puts. You'll need:

- A **margin or individual account** that has **options approval**.

- You do *not* need advanced trading clearance — just **Level 1 or Level 2 options approval** (depending on the broker).

Tip: If you already have the account you used for the strategies in **Covered Calls for Working People***, you're almost ready to go. Just double-check your approval level and cash balance.*

Cash Balance

When you sell a cash-secured put, your broker requires you to **set aside enough cash** to cover the potential purchase of 100 shares at the strike price.

Example:

- Strike price = $50

- One option contract = 100 shares

- Cash required = $5,000

This is why it's called "cash-secured." The broker literally holds that money in reserve.

Options Approval Levels

Each broker has slightly different wording, but here's what to look for:

- **Level 1:** Covered calls (and sometimes cash-secured puts).

- **Level 2:** Cash-secured puts are almost always included here.

- **Level 3 and higher:** Advanced strategies (naked puts, spreads, iron condors, etc.) — not required for this book.

If you're not sure what level you have, log in to your broker's platform, check your **account settings**, and look for "options trading approval."

IRA Accounts

Yes—you can often sell cash-secured puts in an IRA, because the position is considered "safe" (cash is reserved). Some brokers allow it, some don't. If you want to use retirement accounts, ask your broker directly.

Taxes and Records

Just like in *Covered Calls for Working People*, good record-keeping is critical. Even though the broker provides 1099 forms at tax time, you should still track:

- Strike prices you sell

- Premiums collected

- Expiration dates

- Whether you were assigned shares

Later in this book, I'll provide a simple **tracker template** (similar to the one in my covered call book) so you can keep everything organized.

Bottom Line

You don't need anything fancy — just:

1. A brokerage account with basic options approval.

2. Enough cash to cover the puts you sell.

3. A simple system for tracking trades and premiums.

Once these are in place, you're ready to step into the world of cash-secured puts.

If you've already read *Covered Calls for Working People*, think of this as the **mirror image strategy**. Covered calls start with stock you already own. Cash-secured puts start with the cash you're willing to invest. Together, they form the full Wheel Strategy.

Chapter 3: Choosing the Right Stocks for Cash-Secured Puts

One of the most important decisions you'll make with cash-secured puts is **which stock to trade.** The strategy itself is simple — you collect premium and either keep the cash or buy shares at a discount. But if you choose the wrong stock, you could end up owning something you don't actually want.

Just like in *Covered Calls for Working People*, stock selection makes all the difference. Covered calls work best on stable, dividend-paying, or quality growth stocks you don't mind holding. The same applies here — because there's always a chance you'll be assigned.

(With that said, I personally make some covered calls and cash secured puts on a couple volatile stocks. The premiums tend to be higher, and if you are not averse to the risk then give it a shot if you want.)

The Golden Rule

Only sell cash-secured puts on stocks you'd be willing to own.
If you don't like the company, the balance sheet, or the long-term outlook, don't sell a put on it.

5 Criteria for CSP Stock Selection

1. **Quality Business**

   o Choose companies you understand.

   o Look for stable revenue, strong brands, and consistent earnings.

   o Examples: Apple, Microsoft, Coca-Cola.

2. **Reasonable Price Range**

   o Avoid super-high-priced stocks (like $400+) unless your account is large.

   o Remember: one contract = 100 shares. A $400 stock requires $40,000 cash.

3. **Liquidity**

   o Make sure the options market is active.

   o Look for **tight bid-ask spreads** (difference between buy and sell price of the option).

   o The more liquid the option, the easier it is to enter and exit.

4. **Premium vs. Risk Balance**

   o Higher volatility = higher premiums, but also higher risk.

   o Balance is key. Don't chase the fattest premium if the stock itself is unstable.

5. **Avoiding Event Landmines**

   o Be careful around earnings announcements or big news events.

o A stock can swing 10–20% overnight on earnings, which can wipe out your plan.

Example: Safe vs. Risky CSP Choices

- **Safe Choice:** Coca-Cola (KO) at $60. You'd be happy to own 100 shares if assigned, and while you wait, you collect premium.

- **Risky Choice:** A small biotech stock at $7 with huge volatility. The premium looks juicy, but the company could drop 50% on bad news.

The Covered Call Connection

In *Covered Calls for Working People*, we focused on the importance of picking stocks that are worth holding for the long run. With CSPs, that principle is even more important. If you're assigned, you'll own 100 shares. And once you have those shares, you can **immediately sell covered calls** on them — turning a put trade into a full Wheel Strategy cycle.

Quick Checklist Before Selling a CSP

- Do I understand the business?

- Am I comfortable owning 100 shares?

- Is the option liquid with tight spreads?

- Is the premium worth the risk?

- Is there an earnings report or big news coming up?

If you can check all those boxes, you've got a candidate.

Bottom Line

Stock selection is your **first line of defense**. With good choices, CSPs can feel like "getting paid to wait" for the stocks you want anyway. With bad choices, you could end up stuck with shares you regret buying.

Take the time to be selective. It's better to sell fewer puts on quality names than to chase high premiums on weak ones.

Chapter 4: Strike Price & Expiration Selection

Once you've picked a stock you'd be happy to own, the next step is deciding **which strike price and expiration date** to use. This is where you balance income, safety, and probability of success.

Just like in *Covered Calls for Working People*, where you had to choose a strike for your covered call, the same decision-making applies here — only in reverse. With covered calls, you picked a price you were willing to sell your stock. With cash-secured puts, you pick a price you're willing to buy stock.

Strike Price Basics

The **strike price** is the price at which you might be required to buy the stock.

- Choose a **lower strike price** than the stock's current price if you want a safer trade.

- Choose a **strike closer to current price** if you want more premium but more chance of being assigned.

Rule of Thumb: Pick a strike price where you'd say, *"Yes, I'd happily own 100 shares at this level."*

Expiration Basics

The **expiration date** is how long the option contract lasts.

- Shorter expirations (1–2 weeks): smaller premiums but faster turnarounds.

- Longer expirations (1–2 months): bigger premiums but slower cycles.

Most CSP traders stick to **2–4 weeks out**, which provides a balance of income and flexibility.

The Delta Shortcut

If you've read my covered call book, you'll remember "delta" as a way to measure probabilities. The same applies here.

- **Delta ~0.30:** About a 70% chance the option expires worthless (you keep premium, no shares assigned).

- **Delta ~0.50:** About a 50/50 chance of being assigned.

- **Delta ~0.10:** Safer, but premiums are small.

You don't have to obsess over delta, but it helps you quickly gauge risk vs reward.

Example: Picking a Strike & Expiration

Stock: Microsoft (MSFT) trading at $330.

- **Choice A (Conservative):** Sell the $320 strike put expiring in 2 weeks for $2.50 premium ($250).

  - High chance of expiring worthless.

  - If assigned, you buy at $320 instead of $330.

- **Choice B (Aggressive):** Sell the $330 strike put expiring in 2 weeks for $6 premium ($600).

  - More income, but higher chance of assignment.

  - If assigned, you own at $330, minus $6 premium = $324 effective cost.

Both are valid — the key is aligning with your comfort level.

How This Connects to Covered Calls

In *Covered Calls for Working People*, you learned that strike selection determines whether you keep your stock or sell it at a profit. Here, strike selection determines whether you keep your cash or buy stock at a discount. Together, the two choices form the wheel:

- Sell a put to *enter* a stock.

- Sell a call to *exit* a stock.

Quick Checklist for Strike & Expiration

- Am I comfortable owning the stock at this strike?

- Is the expiration far enough out to pay well, but not so far that I'm locked in?

- Does the delta line up with my risk tolerance?

- Is the premium worth tying up my cash?

Bottom Line

Picking strike and expiration is a balance. If you want safer trades, pick lower strikes and shorter expirations. If you want more premium, pick closer strikes or longer expirations. There's no one right answer — only the one that matches your risk, cash, and comfort.

With practice, you'll develop a rhythm. And once you understand how strikes and expirations affect your income, you'll see just how powerful cash-secured puts can be.

Chapter 5: Placing Your First Trade

By now, you understand what a cash-secured put is, how to pick a stock, and how to choose your strike and expiration. Let's put it all together with a walkthrough of placing your first trade.

Don't worry — this is not complicated. In fact, it's very similar to the process you've already used if you've ever bought or sold a stock. The difference is that instead of clicking **Buy Stock**, you'll be choosing **Sell to Open Put Option**.

Step 1: Open Your Brokerage Platform

- Log into your broker (Fidelity, Schwab, TD Ameritrade, Robinhood, etc.).

- Pull up the stock's option chain (the list of all available puts and calls).

- Make sure you're looking at the **Put** side.

Step 2: Pick Strike and Expiration

From Chapter 4, you already know how to select these. For example:

- Stock price: $3.50 (Opendoor, ticker OPEN).

- You believe $3 is a fair entry point.

- You look at the $3 strike, expiring in 1 week.

- Premium being offered: $0.20 per share, or $20 per contract.

I've personally used Opendoor puts this way to either collect cash or enter the stock below market price.

Step 3: Enter the Order

- Order type: **Sell to Open**.

- Quantity: 1 contract = 100 shares.

- Strike: $3.00.

- Expiration: 1 week out.

- Premium (limit order): $0.20.

Your screen will usually show something like this:

"Sell to Open 1 Put, OPEN, $3 strike, expiring [date], Limit $0.20."

Step 4: Confirm the Cash Requirement

Before you hit submit, check the broker's cash requirement.

- $3 strike × 100 shares = $300 cash required.

- This cash will be "set aside" until the contract expires or is closed.

- You'll see it in your account as **cash held for options collateral.**

Step 5: Place the Trade

Click **Submit** (or **Review & Place** depending on your broker). Once filled, you immediately receive the premium. In our example: $20 cash deposited.

Step 6: Manage the Position

Now you wait until expiration:

1. **If OPEN stays above $3.** Your option expires worthless. You keep the $20, and your $300 cash is released.

2. **If OPEN drops below $3.** You're assigned 100 shares at $3. Cost = $300, but you already collected $20. Your effective cost is $2.80 per share.

This is how I've managed some of my own OPEN trades — sometimes I never got assigned, sometimes I did, and either way I was happy. If I was assigned, I'd move to the next step of the Wheel and sell a covered call (as I explained in *Covered Calls for Working People*).

The Bigger Picture

Once you've placed one CSP, you'll realize it's not mysterious at all. It's just like placing a stock order, but with the added benefit of being paid up front. The hardest part isn't the mechanics — it's having the patience to pick the right stock and strike, and the discipline to follow your plan.

Bottom Line

Placing a cash-secured put is a five-minute process once you've chosen your setup. The income is immediate, the risk is defined, and if you're assigned shares, you own a stock you wanted at a discount.

Chapter 6: Managing the Position

One of the best parts about cash-secured puts is that there are really only a few possible outcomes. If you know what to do in each situation, you'll never feel stuck. Think of this as your **troubleshooting guide**.

📌 Scenario 1: The Put Expires Worthless

What happened:

- Stock stayed above your strike price through expiration.
- No one exercises the option.

Result:

- You keep 100% of the premium.
- Your cash is released back into your account.

Next step:

- Sell another cash-secured put on the same stock, or move to another candidate.
- This is the "rinse and repeat" part of the strategy.

📌 Scenario 2: The Put Is Assigned (You Buy Shares)

What happened:

- Stock closed below your strike price at expiration.
- You're required to buy 100 shares at the strike.

Result:

- You own the stock at strike price.

- Your effective cost is strike – premium collected.

Next step:

- If you like the stock, this is exactly what you wanted.

- Now you can move to the second half of the Wheel: **sell a covered call** against those shares.

- As I explained in *Covered Calls for Working People*, this lets you collect even more premium while you wait for the stock to move.

📌 Scenario 3: The Put Is In-the-Money but Not Assigned Yet

What happened:

- Stock has fallen below strike price before expiration.

- But you haven't been assigned yet (assignment can happen any day before expiration).

Result:

- Your option has value.

- You can choose to wait, or close early.

Next step options:

1. **Do nothing** → If you're happy owning shares, let it play out.

2. **Buy to close the option** → Lock in a smaller loss or reduce risk.

3. **Roll the option forward** → Close the current put and open a new one with a later expiration or different strike.

📌 Scenario 4: The Stock Drops Hard Below Strike

What happened:

- The stock collapsed far below your strike.

- Example: You sold a $50 put, stock is now at $40.

Result:

- You will almost certainly be assigned at expiration.

- Your effective cost basis is still strike – premium, but you're underwater on the shares.

Next step options:

- **If it's a quality stock:** Accept the assignment, then sell covered calls while you wait for recovery.

- **If fundamentals have changed:** Consider closing early for a loss and moving to a better stock.

This is where discipline matters. Remember the rule from Chapter 3: only sell puts on stocks you're willing to own. If you stuck to that, assignment isn't a disaster — it's a discount entry point.

📌 Scenario 5: You Want to Free Up Cash Before Expiration

What happened:

- You sold a put but now need the cash back before expiration (maybe for another opportunity).

Result:

- You're still obligated until you close the trade.

Next step:

- Place a **Buy to Close** order on the put.

- If the option lost value (stock went up), you'll close for a profit.

- If the option gained value (stock went down), you'll pay more to close, but at least your cash is freed up.

Quick Reference Flow

- Stock above strike → Keep premium → Sell another put.

- Stock slightly below strike → Assigned shares → Sell covered call.

- Stock far below strike → Decide: hold quality stock or cut losses.

- Need cash back → Buy to close anytime.

Bottom Line

Managing cash-secured puts isn't about predicting the market. It's about knowing what to do when each scenario happens. If you keep it simple, you'll always have a plan: either you keep your premium, or you buy stock you already wanted.

And once you own those shares, you're back in familiar territory: **covered calls** — the very strategy I taught step by step in *Covered Calls* *for Working People*. Together, these two books give you the tools to run the entire Wheel Strategy.

Chapter 7: Risks & Mistakes to Avoid

Cash-secured puts are simple, but that doesn't mean they're foolproof. Many beginners make the same mistakes, and it costs them money or discourages them before they even get started. Here are the top 10 pitfalls to avoid.

1. Selling Puts on Stocks You Don't Want to Own

If you wouldn't buy 100 shares of the stock outright, don't sell a put on it.

Covered Calls for Working People taught you to choose quality stocks for calls. The same principle applies here.

2. Chasing the Biggest Premiums

High premiums usually mean high volatility. That juicy $2.50 option on a $10 stock may look great — until the stock tanks 50%.

Premiums are only good if the underlying stock is worth owning.

3. Ignoring Earnings Announcements

Earnings can move a stock 10–20% overnight. Don't sell puts right before earnings unless you're 100% willing to own at a much lower price.

4. Overcommitting Cash

Each contract ties up real money (strike × 100). If you sell too many puts, you'll run out of flexibility — and possibly face a margin call.

Always leave room to manage trades or roll forward.

5. Forgetting to Track Trades

You'll collect premiums, but if you don't record strike prices, expirations, and outcomes, you'll lose track fast.

Use the simple trade log I included here (and similar to the one in my covered call book).

6. Rolling Without a Plan

Rolling puts can be useful, but beginners often roll just to delay taking a loss. If you don't understand *why* you're rolling, you're just kicking the can down the road.

7. Selling Strikes Too Close to the Money

It's tempting to sell at-the-money puts for big premiums, but that increases the odds of assignment. If you don't want shares immediately, pick safer strikes further out of the money.

8. Ignoring the Bigger Market Trend

If the whole market is dropping, even the best stock can get pulled down. Don't treat puts as if they're immune to market conditions.

9. Thinking It's Risk-Free

CSPs are safer than naked puts, but they're not risk-free. If the stock collapses, you'll own shares at a loss. Don't risk money you can't afford to invest long term.

---

10. Not Using the Covered Call Exit

If you're assigned stock, don't just sit on it doing nothing. Turn those shares into an income engine by selling covered calls — the strategy I walked through in *Covered Calls for Working People*. This is how you complete the Wheel and keep generating cash.

Bottom Line

Most of these mistakes come down to discipline. Don't chase, don't rush, don't overextend. Stick to quality stocks, smart strikes, and the simple rules in this book, and CSPs can be a reliable, low-stress part of your investing toolkit.

Chapter 8: Real-World Case Studies

Theory is helpful, but nothing beats walking through real examples. In this chapter, we'll look at three different cash-secured put trades: one on a smaller, volatile stock (*Opendoor*), one on a steady dividend stock (*Coca-Cola*), and one on a big tech growth stock (*Microsoft*). These case studies show you the variety of outcomes you can expect — and how to handle each one.

Case Study 1: Opendoor (OPEN) — Small Cap, High Volatility

- **Stock Price:** $3.50

- **Trade:** Sell $3.00 put, 1 week out, premium = $0.20 per share ($20).

- **Cash Requirement:** $300.

Outcome A (Stock stays above $3):

- OPEN closes at $3.25.

- Put expires worthless.

- Profit = $20, cash released.

- Annualized yield (if repeated): surprisingly high because of small capital requirement.

Outcome B (Stock drops below $3):

- OPEN falls to $2.80.

- Assigned 100 shares at $3 ($300).

- Effective cost = $2.80 ($3 − $0.20).

- Now you own shares. Next step = sell covered calls at $3.50 or $4 for additional premium.

Lesson: Small-cap stocks like OPEN provide higher percentage returns, but the risk of assignment is higher too. You must be comfortable owning shares and possibly sitting on them until the market recovers.

Case Study 2: Coca-Cola (KO) — Dividend Blue Chip

- **Stock Price:** $60.

- **Trade:** Sell $57.50 put, 4 weeks out, premium = $1.00 per share ($100).

- **Cash Requirement:** $5,750.

Outcome A (Stock stays above $57.50):

- KO closes at $59.

- Put expires worthless.

- Profit = $100, which is ~1.7% return on cash in just 4 weeks.

Outcome B (Stock drops below $57.50):

- KO falls to $56.

- Assigned 100 shares at $57.50 ($5,750).

- Effective cost = $56.50 ($57.50 – $1.00).

- You now own a solid dividend stock at a discount. Next step = sell covered calls at $60 while collecting dividends.

Lesson: With steady companies, assignment isn't scary — you end up with quality stock you'd likely hold anyway.

Case Study 3: Microsoft (MSFT) — Large-Cap Tech Growth

- **Stock Price:** $330.

- **Trade:** Sell $320 put, 2 weeks out, premium = $2.50 per share ($250).

- **Cash Requirement:** $32,000.

Outcome A (Stock stays above $320):

- MSFT closes at $335.

- Put expires worthless.

- Profit = $250, cash released.

Outcome B (Stock drops below $320):

- MSFT falls to $318.

- Assigned 100 shares at $320 ($32,000).

- Effective cost = $317.50 ($320 – $2.50).

- You now own Microsoft at a small discount. Next step = sell covered calls at $330–$335 for $3–$4 per share, generating more income.

Lesson: Large-cap tech trades tie up more capital, but they offer steady premium opportunities. If assigned, you own a world-class company at a slight discount.

Pulling It Together

Across these three examples, you've seen the CSP outcomes:

- **Expire worthless:** you keep the premium, and your cash is freed.

- **Assigned shares:** you buy stock at a discount and can transition to covered calls.

- **Different stock types behave differently:** smaller stocks give higher % returns but more risk, while blue chips and tech giants provide steady, safer plays.

As you gain experience, you'll find your own sweet spot — whether that's safer dividend names, high-growth tech, or occasional small-cap plays.

And remember: if you've read *Covered Calls for Working People*, you already know what to do with assigned shares. Covered calls are the natural next step in the Wheel Strategy, and together with CSPs, they give you a full system for generating monthly income.

Chapter 9: Taxes & Record-Keeping

Trading cash-secured puts is simple — until tax time, when you have to sort out what happened. If you keep good records along the way, you'll save yourself hours of stress later.

Just like in *Covered Calls for Working People*, I recommend building a simple log for every trade. Don't rely only on your broker's year-end statement. Brokers will give you the raw data, but they don't explain your thought process, outcomes, or Wheel Strategy flow. That's why your own record-keeping matters.

Why Keep Records?

- **Taxes:** In the U.S., option premiums and stock sales show up on your 1099, but it's much easier to reconcile if you tracked each trade.

- **Learning:** Reviewing your log teaches you what worked and what didn't.

- **Planning:** Helps you see monthly income and realistic annual returns.

What to Track

At minimum, record these items for every CSP trade:

- **Date opened**

- **Ticker symbol**

- **Strike price**

- **Expiration date**

- **Premium received**

- **Cash required**

- **Outcome (expired worthless, assigned, closed early, rolled, etc.)**

- **Notes** (Why you chose it, or what you'll do next — e.g., sell covered call).

- **Tax Notes (U.S. Focus)**

- **Premiums:** Count as short-term capital gains in the year received.

- **Assigned shares:** Premium reduces your cost basis. (e.g., assigned at $50 with $2 premium = $48 basis).

- **Expired worthless:** Premium is kept as short-term capital gains.

- **Rolled trades:** Premiums are combined — each adjustment adds to your net credit or debit.

Disclaimer reminder: This is not tax advice. Always confirm with a licensed tax professional.

Bottom Line

- Keeping a log transforms CSPs from a casual trade into a real system. It not only keeps you ready for tax season, but also gives you a clear picture of your monthly cash flow.

- *In my own journey, I've kept a simple spreadsheet since my early covered call days (as I described in **Covered Calls for Working People**). That same habit works perfectly here for CSPs.*

Chapter 10: Next Steps & Conclusion

You've now seen how cash-secured puts work, how to pick stocks, choose strikes, manage outcomes, and avoid common mistakes. By this point, you should realize that CSPs aren't complicated — they're just a disciplined way of getting paid to wait for the right stock at the right price.

Where to Go from Here

1. **Practice Small**
   Start with one put on a stock you're already comfortable with. Don't rush into selling multiple contracts until you understand how it feels to manage one.

2. **Build a Routine**
   Each month, look at your watchlist. Sell a put or two. Record the trade. Let the results play out. This slow, steady rhythm is what makes the strategy work over time.

3. **Think in Terms of the Wheel**
   Remember, CSPs are the first half of the Wheel Strategy. If assigned, you own the stock. At that point, the natural next step is to sell covered calls — exactly what I laid out in *Covered Calls for Working People*. Together, these two books give you the full cycle.

4. **Stay Disciplined**
   Avoid chasing big premiums, don't overload your account, and always stick to stocks you'd be happy to own. If you keep those rules in mind, you'll avoid most beginner pitfalls.

The Big Picture

Cash-secured puts aren't a get-rich-quick scheme. They're a methodical way to:

- Generate extra cash flow.

- Enter stocks at better prices.

- Build a long-term portfolio with income along the way.

When combined with covered calls, you have the tools to run the full Wheel Strategy — a system that can generate steady monthly income whether the market is flat, rising, or slowly drifting down.

Final Word

My hope is that this book gave you not just the mechanics of cash-secured puts, but also the confidence to try them yourself. The more you practice, the more natural it becomes.

Thank you for reading, and if you haven't already, I encourage you to check out my companion book, *Covered Calls for Working People*. Together, these two strategies are like the left and right wheels of the same cart — and once they're turning, they can carry you toward consistent income and financial stability.

— Adrian Gregory

About the Author

Adrian Gregory is an entrepreneur, writer, and self-taught investor with a passion for making finance simple for everyday people. After years of studying the markets on his own, Adrian discovered the power of covered calls — a strategy that creates steady income from stocks without the need for risky speculation.

He believes that anyone, no matter their background or account size, can learn to make their money work harder with straightforward strategies explained in plain English.

When he isn't trading or writing, Adrian runs a braille transcription business dedicated to accessibility, designs puzzles and books, and spends time with his wife and daughters in Tennessee.

You can connect with Adrian and follow his ongoing insights at his Substack newsletter: **Adrian / @adrian716731**

Glossary of Terms

Assignment: When the option seller (you) is required to buy the stock at the strike price because the option buyer exercised their right.

At the Money (ATM): An option whose strike price is very close to the current stock price.

Bid: The highest price a buyer is willing to pay for an option.

Ask (Offer): The lowest price a seller is willing to accept for an option.

Brokerage Account: The account you open with a brokerage firm (like Robinhood, Fidelity, Schwab, etc.) to trade stocks and options.

Cash-Secured Put: An options strategy where you sell a put option and keep enough cash in your account to buy the stock if assigned.

Collateral: The cash set aside in your account to cover the possible stock purchase from a sold put.

Covered Call: A related strategy where you sell call options against stock you already own.

Exercise: The act of using the right in an option contract to buy (call) or sell (put) the underlying stock at the strike price.

Expiration Date: The last day an option contract can be exercised.

Extrinsic Value (Time Value): The portion of an option's price that comes from time until expiration and market expectations, not from the stock's current price.

In the Money (ITM): For a put option, this means the stock price is below the strike price.

Liquidity: How easily an option or stock can be bought or sold without causing large price changes. High liquidity usually means tighter bid-ask spreads.

Margin Requirement: The minimum funds required in your account by the broker to back your trades.

Option Contract: A standardized agreement giving the buyer the right (but not the obligation) to buy or sell 100 shares of stock at a specific price, before or at a set date.

Option Premium: The price received (if selling) or paid (if buying) for an option contract.

Out of the Money (OTM): For a put option, this means the stock price is above the strike price.

Return on Capital (ROC): The percentage return earned based on the cash you set aside (collateral) for a cash-secured put.

Rolling an Option: Closing an existing option position and opening a new one at a later date or different strike.

Spread: The difference between the bid and ask price of an option. Narrow spreads usually mean better trading conditions.

Strike Price: The price at which the option buyer can buy (calls) or sell (puts) the stock.

Theta (Time Decay): The rate at which an option loses value as it gets closer to expiration.

Underlying Stock: The specific stock that an option contract is based on.

Volatility: A measure of how much a stock's price is expected to move. Higher volatility usually means higher option premiums.

Writing an Option: Selling an option contract (in this case, selling a put).

For additional trading mistakes and brokerage breakdowns, refer back to the appendices in *Covered Calls for Working People*.

www.ingramcontent.com/pod-product-compliance
Lightning Source LLC
Chambersburg PA
CBHW071522210326
41597CB00018B/2848